PROTECTING THE PLANET

COLIN HARRIS

Wayland

Young Geographer

The Changing Earth
Food and Farming
Journeys
Natural Resources
Protecting the Planet
Settlements
The World's Population
The World's Weather

Series editor: Sarah Doughty
Book editor: Paul Bennett
Designer: Mark Whitchurch
Consultant: Dr Tony Binns, geography lecturer at Sussex
   University

Front cover picture: Divers carrying out tests on a coral reef.
Back cover picture: A crowd in Hawaii, protesting about the
   destruction of the rainforests.
Frontispiece: Poppies and daisies in a meadow in Italy.

First published in 1992 by
Wayland (Publishers) Ltd
61 Western Road, Hove
East Sussex BN3 1JD, England

British Library Cataloguing in Publication Data
Harris, Colin
   Protecting the Planet. – (Young
   Geographer Series)
   I. Title. II. Series
   333.7

ISBN 0 7502 0441 9

Typeset by Type Study, Scarborough, England
Printed in Italy by Rotolito Lombarda S.p.A
Bound in France by A.G.M.

National Curriculum Attainment Targets

This book is most directly relevant to the following
Attainment Targets in the Geography National Curriculum
at Key Stage 2. The information can help in the following
ways:

Attainment Target 2 (Knowledge and understanding of
places) To describe how the landscape of a locality has been
changed by human actions.

Attainment Target 5 (Environmental geography) To
describe the ways in which people have changed the
environment; to discuss ways people look after and improve
their environment; to look at whether some types of
environment need special protection; to describe how
people obtain materials from the ground and the effects of
extracting natural resources; to distinguish between
renewable and non-renewable resources; to identify the
main sources of water; to explain why rivers, lakes, seas and
oceans are vulnerable to pollution, and to describe the ways
in which pollution problems have been addressed.

Contents

All the words that are in **bold** appear in the glossary on page 30.

Introduction

We all know that we have to look after the things that belong to us. If you have a bicycle you know what happens if you leave it out in the rain. If you own a goldfish, you know what happens if you forget to feed it. Everything we care about needs to be looked after.

Have you ever thought about who looks after the world around us? It really belongs to everybody, and so up to all of us to help look after it.

There are some people who do care for the **environment**. They build houses that look attractive, create beautiful gardens, plant trees or care for animals.

Unfortunately, people can also spoil the world around us. They do this by destroying forests, poisoning rivers, overgrazing land or growing too many crops. We all destroy a little of our world by using up its precious **natural resources**,

People have been careless and allowed all this rubbish to be left on a beautiful beach.

These people are helping to care for the environment by clearing a river of muck and rubbish.

such as timber, gas or metals, which cannot easily be replaced. Perhaps you have seen the world around you spoilt in some of these ways.

Perhaps you have also seen some of the ways in which the natural environment is being maintained or improved. Near where you live there may be a nature **reserve**, game reserve, **national park** or wildlife park. These are places where wildlife and the beauty of nature are protected.

People might be damaging our world, but we can begin to put that right. Plan something in your school or in your area – you do not need to leave it all to other people.

Protecting environments

Imagine how dull the world would be if everywhere looked the same. In fact, there is a rich variety of **landscape**, such as high mountains, vast plains, hot deserts and lush forests. People, wild animals and plants can be found in nearly all these places. They are some of the world's environments. Can you think of any others?

The word 'environment' means 'surroundings', and is often used to describe where people live. The environment is made up of the soil, rock, water, plants and air which surround us. We also use the word environment for places where very few people live, such as the ice-sheet of Antarctica.

The Earth is the place where we all live, so if one part of our planet is harmed, it affects all of us. We can help to protect the environment where we live and understand other environments, even if they are a long way away from us. The world's grasslands, wetlands and tropical rainforests all need protection.

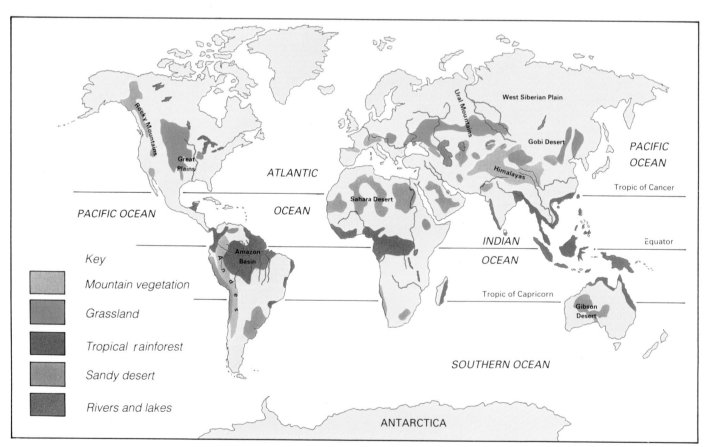

A map showing some of the environments that need protection.

Across North America, the Great Plains are among the world's most important grasslands. They are mostly used for grazing animals, but if farmers plough them to grow crops when there is too little rain, the soil will blow away and the grassland will be destroyed.

The meadows of Europe are rich with wild flowers. If the meadows are dug up, or if certain chemicals are used on them, the flowers will be destroyed. By protecting grassland in North America and Europe, they will be saved.

It is important for farmers to be able to grow food and rear animals, such as cattle, for themselves and for others. But if they grow too

Above Rock, stone and sand make up the natural environment of this desert in Egypt.

Right Fields of maize in Iowa, USA. Farmers must take care not to overwork the land.

much food or keep too many cattle, the land may become overworked or the grass destroyed. When this happens, the land takes many years to recover. In some areas of the world, such as parts of Africa, overfarmed land may turn into deserts or be **eroded** by heavy rain.

Some environments are naturally wet, such as swamps, marshes and bogs. People might want to drain these areas so that they can be developed, but the wetlands of the world contain rare animals and plants and, therefore, need to be protected. For example, alligators depend for their survival on the undisturbed wetlands of the Everglades in Florida. To protect the alligators the Everglades must be left alone.

In Europe the salt marsh coasts of England and the Netherlands are home to rare plants and a wide variety of nesting birds. If they are drained and built on, the plants will disappear and the birds will have nowhere to nest.

A salt marsh in the Netherlands. The wetlands of Europe are home for many plants and birds.

Saving the rainforests

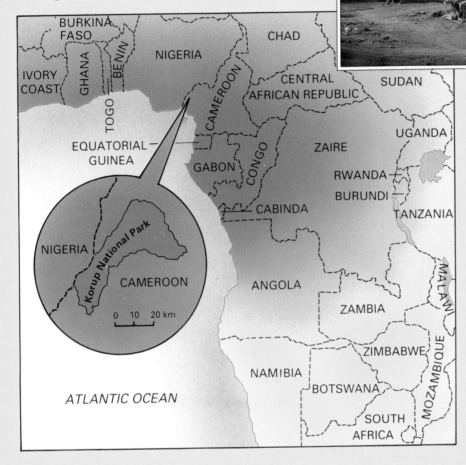

BURKINA FASO
IVORY COAST
GHANA
TOGO
BENIN
NIGERIA
CHAD
CAMEROON
CENTRAL AFRICAN REPUBLIC
SUDAN
EQUATORIAL GUINEA
GABON
CONGO
ZAIRE
UGANDA
RWANDA
BURUNDI
CABINDA
TANZANIA
ANGOLA
ZAMBIA
MALAWI
MOZAMBIQUE
ZIMBABWE
NAMIBIA
BOTSWANA
SOUTH AFRICA
ATLANTIC OCEAN

NIGERIA
Korup National Park
CAMEROON
0 10 20 km

Above *A rainforest village in the Korup National Park.*

Left *A map showing the position of Korup National Park in Cameroon.*

Tropical rainforests are found in South America, Africa and parts of Asia, such as Indonesia and Borneo. Large areas of forest are being cut down to make way for roads, towns, factories and cattle ranches.

Some governments, such as that of Cameroon in West Africa, have realized how important the forests are and are trying to save them. The Korup National Park has been set up in south-west Cameroon. It has about 1,600 sq km of rainforest with six villages in the park.

The people who live in the park are allowed to clear small areas of the forest to grow food. Every year part of the land is rested before growing new crops. The people also hunt wild animals for food, but few animals now remain and so the hunting must stop.

Protecting wildlife

Individual **species** of plants and animals usually occupy only small areas of the Earth's environments. The places where animals and plants live are called habitats. Both animals and plants depend on their habitats for survival, so if we wish to protect wildlife we must also protect their habitats.

Animals will suffer if their habitats are destroyed. Every spring for instance, frogs return to the same pond to lay their eggs, or spawn. If the pond dries up or is drained to make way for a road or building, the frogs have nowhere to spawn and no tadpoles are hatched. In just a few years, there will be no frogs left.

This elephant in Chobe National Park, Botswana, has been killed by ivory poachers for its tusks.

Protecting animals

In northern Canada, the Inuit people have for centuries earned a living by trapping animals such as the muskrat, which have thick fur to protect them against the cold.

In recent years, groups such as Greenpeace and Animal Rights have campaigned successfully against the killing of animals just for their fur. As a result, fewer fur coats are being made and the Inuit, and others, have found other ways of earning money.

The Inuit are changing their way of life to protect the environment. They are now welcoming visitors to the Arctic shores of Canada with their many bays and islands.

Many Inuit have changed their traditional hunting ways and now welcome tourists to their northern Canada homes.

The beautiful, unspoilt forests and lakes are ideal for those tourists who want to discover a part of the world that is still a wilderness.

Similarly, butterflies will only survive if their caterpillars have plants to eat, and the butterflies have flowering plants to feed on. In parts of Europe, the swallowtail butterfly is rare. It needs milk parsley plants on which to lay its eggs. If the habitat of the milk parsley is not protected, the swallowtail will not survive. Do you know of any animals and, possibly, plants that need protection near to where you live?

There are many other wild animals that are under threat. Their plight is highlighted by television and magazines. In Africa, for instance, elephants were endangered because of poachers killing them for their ivory tusks. The trade in ivory is now banned, and the elephants are increasing in numbers again. In fact, there may soon be too many of them in parts of Africa, such as Botswana, so the elephants may now be **culled**.

Animals that once roamed in large numbers can become rare species. At one time in the USA hundreds of thousands of bison (North American buffalo) roamed the Great Plains but, a hundred years ago, they were all but wiped out by hunters using rifles. Today, only two small herds remain, and their habitat will need to be protected if they are to stand any chance of surviving.

Animals in the sea are also at risk. In the Antarctic Ocean, small, shrimp-like creatures called krill are being caught in vast quantities for people to eat. They are the food of many of the penguins that live there. The penguins will disappear if their food supply runs out.

These bison are free to graze in Yellowstone National Park, USA. They are now protected animals.

Tuna fishermen are now being urged to replace these nets with lines and hooks.

Some species of dolphin are disappearing fast because they are being caught in huge nets cast by fishermen to catch tuna. Because of the concern over the dolphins, in some parts of the world the fishermen are being urged to use fishing lines with hooks instead.

These are just a few of the animals across the world that are in danger, but there are many more. In every continent, as a result of people destroying habitats and killing animals, many species of plants and animals are threatened with **extinction**.

Water pollution

The word 'pollution' describes what happens when the natural world becomes spoilt. Air is polluted by soot, smoke and poisonous gases. Water is polluted when we allow poisonous or dirty substances to enter it.

It is important that we have clean and pure water. When our water supply becomes polluted, it can make us ill. The water we drink comes from rivers, wells and **boreholes**. Scientists regularly check our water supplies to make sure that they are safe to drink. In some countries, water of any sort is scarce. In parts of Africa and India, for example, people have to travel many kilometres to find water, and even then it may be dirty.

This well supplies water for a whole village in Rajasthan, India.

Healthy ponds contain many plants and animals. This woman is checking the water for pollution.

Rivers can become polluted if chemical **pesticides** sprayed on crops and **fertilizers** added to soils are washed into rivers. Factories and power stations may also pour waste into rivers, which kills fish and eventually all other forms of river life. Polluted rivers and streams look dirty and may also smell unpleasant.

Rivers, lakes and seas can also be polluted if we allow our toilets to be flushed into them without the waste being treated. The raw **sewage** can carry the tiny organisms that cause disease. In some **tropical** countries, fresh water spoilt by raw sewage may contain the tiny grubs of small worms that cause the life-threatening disease bilharzia.

Seas and oceans make up more than two-thirds of the total area of the Earth's surface. Pollution of the oceans can be caused when oil from tankers is poured into them, and when waste from our homes and factories is carried away in underground pipes. These take the waste straight to the sea without being treated first to remove harmful sewage and chemicals.

It is easy to see why we allow waste to be poured into the seas and oceans. They are so vast it appears that a little pollution may not be harmful. However, the seas and oceans are harmed every time waste is dumped into them. When raw sewage is pumped out to sea, it builds up into harmful silt, which spoils our beaches, kills wildlife, and can be a threat to health.

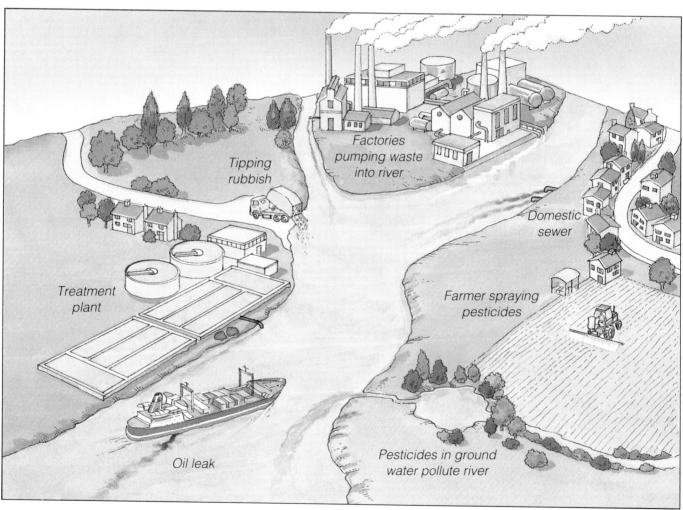

Some of the ways that rivers and lakes can become polluted.

Willamette River, Oregon

Twenty-five years ago, the Willamette River in Oregon was one of the most polluted rivers in the USA. Household sewage and waste from industry caused most of the pollution, making the river ugly and filthy. Salmon and trout could no longer spawn.

People who lived in the towns along the river demanded that something should be done to clear up the pollution. Sewage plants were built and all factories had to treat their wastes before pumping them into the river. This was the first large river in the USA to be cleaned up in this way.

A river in the USA is polluted by a factory. Scenes like this were common on the Willamette River.

Fish have now returned to the river and it is safe for water sports. Also, the banks along the river are being protected to allow camping, boating and other leisure activities.

People using hoses and detergents to clean up an oil slick from a beach at Point St Helens, Alaska. Oil spills at sea can devastate wildlife.

Ocean waters have also been known to be poisoned by deposits of mercury, aluminium and other metals. In Japan, for example, people have been poisoned by mercury after they have eaten fish caught from polluted seas.

Shipwrecked tankers spill millions of barrels of crude oil into the sea, and the pollution kills thousands of fish and sea birds. During the Gulf War in 1991, oil was deliberately poured into the Persian Gulf, harming birds and the wide variety of life on and around coral reefs.

Protecting the atmosphere

In our solar system the Earth is the only planet with an **atmosphere** that can support people, animals and plants. The air around us is very important to us. We feel the air when it moves. If the winds blow to us from a cold place, then we feel cold winds; if they blow from a hot place, then they feel warm. Sometimes the winds carry things with them, such as the fine red dust that falls on southern Britain when winds blow from the Sahara Desert in North Africa.

The air, or atmosphere, contains gases including oxygen, nitrogen and carbon dioxide. We need oxygen in order to breathe, in the same way that plants need carbon dioxide to survive. At present, harmful gases and other substances are being produced by human activity. As a result, the atmosphere is in need of protection.

If this coke-making plant filtered the smoke from its chimneys, the air would be cleaner.

An oil fire in Kuwait. Putting the fires out was very dangerous work.

Oil fires in Kuwait

At the end of the war in the Persian Gulf in 1991, many of the oil wells in Kuwait were set on fire causing terrible air pollution. This could have affected the weather in places as far away as India.

The task of putting out the fires was too great for Kuwait alone, so many other countries helped. One famous fighter of oil fires, the American Red Adair, was one of the first people to arrive on the scene. Even he could not put out the raging fires without help from Britain and other European countries using large fire-fighting machines.

Unfortunately, the gushing oil that fuelled the flames continued to escape for some time and formed large black lakes in the desert sand.

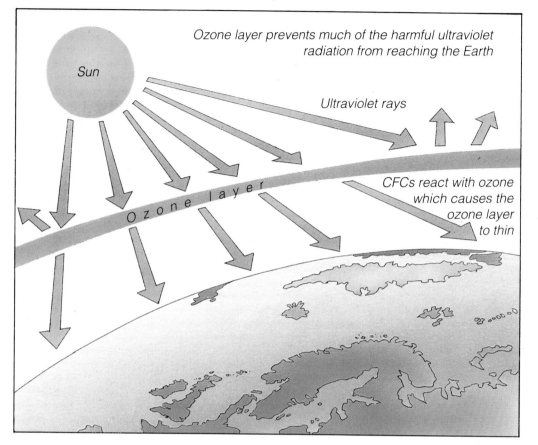

Ozone layer prevents much of the harmful ultraviolet radiation from reaching the Earth

Sun

Ultraviolet rays

O z o n e   l a y e r

CFCs react with ozone which causes the ozone layer to thin

Top right Acid rain in Czechoslovakia has stripped these trees of their leaves.

Right A diagram showing how acid rain is formed.

Left CFCs released into the atmosphere damage the ozone layer and cause it to become thinner.

Cars using leaded petrol cause high levels of harmful lead in the atmosphere. Cars also produce carbon dioxide, which traps heat from the Sun and causes temperatures to rise around the world.

Some **aerosols** and refrigerators cause gases called **CFCs** to be released into the atmosphere. These damage the **ozone layer**, a band of gases which encloses the Earth's atmosphere, and which helps to protect us from harmful rays from the Sun. When fuels like coal and oil are burnt, they produce tiny black particles called soot, which damage the quality of the air.

We can help to protect the atmosphere by using only 'safe' aerosols and by using only diesel fuel or unleaded petrol in our cars. If we have open fires at home, we should burn smokeless fuel and make compost heaps of garden rubbish instead of lighting bonfires. In Britain from 1993 it will be illegal to burn **stubble** left in fields after grain crops, such as wheat and barley, have been harvested.

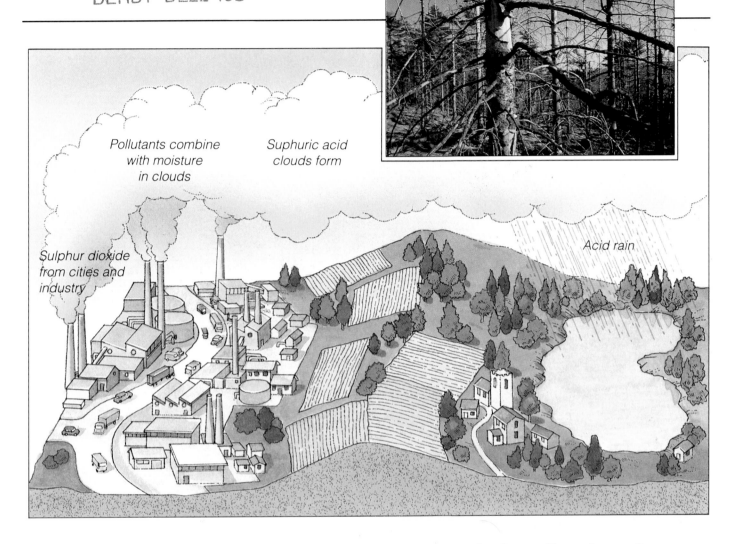

Pollutants combine with moisture in clouds

Suphuric acid clouds form

Sulphur dioxide from cities and industry

Acid rain

While cars pose a major threat to the atmosphere, power stations which generate electricity by burning coal, gas and oil, cause an even greater threat, because of the amount of carbon dioxide and other gases they produce. They also cause **acid rain**, which results from the gas sulphur dioxide being absorbed by moisture in the atmosphere. The acid rain falls on places sometimes hundreds of kilometres away from the power station.

Forests in Scandinavia and Germany are dying from the effects of acid rain produced in Britain and former Eastern European countries, such as East Germany.

Governments as well as individuals must decide what to do in order to protect the atmosphere. Only when certain fuels are banned, or special parts are fitted to chimneys to 'scrub' the gases clean, will there be an improvement to the quality of air.

Conserving natural resources

Every day all of us use up some of the Earth's natural resources. Each time we switch on a light, cook food or go for a ride in a car we are using up the Earth's energy sources.

Some of the resources that we use can be replaced, for instance food, wood and cotton. These are known as renewable resources. Other resources such as coal, oil and natural gas cannot be replaced.

Right The softwood trees on these hillsides were planted as a crop. Fewer animals live here than in forests that have a variety of trees.

Left This area of Western Australia was once covered with forest. After the trees were cut down, the rain washed the soil away.

It is then washed or blown away by rain or winds. As a result, there is no soil to grow new trees in, and the forest becomes like a non-renewable resource.

We use timber for buildings and to make furniture. Hardwood trees, such as oak, beech and mahogany, which grow in tropical or **temperate** forests, grow slowly. Much of the temperate woodland in Europe and North America has been cleared to make way for farms and cities. Although it takes some time, new forests can be created to replace those that have been cut down.

Softwood trees, such as pines, spruces and firs, which are used for making paper, grow more quickly and can, therefore, be renewed easily. But if we plant them in parts

These are called non-renewable resources because they can only be used once.

In some parts of the world, the forests are cut down so that cattle can graze or crops can be grown. But the soil becomes **infertile**.

Industry in northern Russia

On the Kola Peninsula of northern Russia, the nickel industry has devastated the countryside. The ore is mined and the metal smelted, pouring smoke and chemicals on to a landscape as barren as the Moon. There is a strong chemical smell everywhere, trees without leaves, and bare hillsides with dead, twisted tree trunks.

Thousands of people depend on work in the mines and smelters to earn a living. If the factories were closed, there would be nothing else for the people to do. In other parts of the Russian Arctic, people herd reindeer. Compare the work of these people with the work of the people who mine the nickel. One group rely on renewable resources, the other on non-renewable resources. Do you know which is which?

Left Tonnes of sand are dug out of the ground by this huge machine.

of the world where they do not grow as part of the natural vegetation, we may cause problems because they naturally increase soil acidity, making it impossible for native plants to grow.

We use sand and gravel for making roads and erecting buildings. Once the sand and gravel have been removed from the ground, they cannot be replaced.

But there is far more gravel in the world than we shall ever need. However, the digging for sand and gravel makes the landscape ugly, but it can be restored by building nature reserves or recreation parks.

Electricity is usually generated by using non-renewable forms of energy. But the process can also be powered by tidal, wind and solar energy. Electricity generating

Coal mine

Gravel pit

Hydroelectric power

Coal-fired power station

Wind farm

Oil field

Softwood trees

Solar panels

stations, such as the one on the River Rance in northern France, use the power of the rising and falling tide to operate **turbines**.

In parts of California, in the USA, 'wind farms' have dozens of two- or three-bladed wind generators to produce electricity. Houses in many parts of the world are being fitted with roof panels which make use of the energy of the Sun's rays to heat water and warm the house. All these are called **alternative** sources of energy.

Waste and recycling

Every day we throw away things that we do not need any more. These include cans, paper bags, cardboard boxes, glass bottles and plastic cups. Every week, the average family in countries in the developed world throw away about 12 kg of waste. Where does it all go?

Each country has its own way of collecting and **disposing** of its rubbish. If we do not dispose of our waste carefully, we could spoil our environment. Imagine what it would be like if all our rubbish was dumped in the street.

When rubbish is collected and transported, care must be taken to ensure that nothing is blown away in the wind. Lorries and barges have special covers to prevent rubbish escaping. When no care is taken, the rubbish can collect in fields,

Some of the waste that was collected from homes during a campaign called 'Earth Day' in the USA.

At Pitsea, the landfill site is carefully monitored and any leaking, poisonous liquid is pumped away before it can cause damage to the water supply.

Pitsea landfill site, London

In Britain, most of the waste collected each week from homes goes to landfill sites. One site at Pitsea near London covers 4.25 sq km. Every year, 350,000 tonnes of rubbish from London is dumped at Pitsea. Waste from factories is also dumped there, but each load is tested first to make sure no harm will be done to people who live nearby.

Landfill sites are one of the best ways of getting rid of rubbish as long as they are looked after properly. After each day's work, the rubbish is covered with soil to prevent it blowing away. Methane gas at Pitsea escapes safely through pipes, and liquid leaking from the rubbish is carefully checked and is pumped away to a safe place. Do you think the landfill site is an environmentally friendly way to deal with household and industrial rubbish?

hedgerows and woods. The litter is unsightly, and as plastic and glass do not break down, it will remain there until it is picked up.

Most household or domestic rubbish is collected in lorries and taken to landfill sites, where it is dumped into holes in the ground.

When the holes are full, they are covered with soil and restored to fields and woods.

The decaying rubbish gives off a gas called methane. It is a dangerous gas as it can build up and cause an explosion if it is not properly controlled. Methane can also be useful when used as a fuel for heating homes or generating electricity.

In some countries, such as in Denmark, rubbish is burnt in large **incinerators**. What is left after burning is crushed to take up less space, and then taken to a landfill site. Unless the ash is covered by soil, it will be blown in the wind and cause pollution.

Some waste can be recycled, that is, it can be used again. Glass bottles can be thrown into bottle banks.

Waste must be sorted properly before it can be recycled. For example, glass bottles must be separated from plastic ones.

Used cardboard can easily be recycled. It is made into bales like these so that it can be transported with ease.

A lorry will take the bottle-bank containers to a factory where the glass is crushed and made into bottles again. Metals, such as steel scrap are recycled after use. Aluminium cans are crushed by a machine and recycled in large quantities. Other materials that can be recycled include paper, cardboard and clothing.

Recycling materials can be less damaging to the environment than producing new ones. Try and find out about local schemes in your area. You will not only be saving the world's resources, but you also will be cutting down on the amount of energy used and the pollution that often occurs when materials are produced.

Glossary

Acid rain Rain containing pollutants released into the atmosphere by burning fossil fuels.

Aerosols Containers of liquid and gas, from which the liquid is squirted in the form of a mist.

Alternative Offering a second possibility.

Atmosphere The air round the Earth.

Boreholes Holes drilled in the ground in search of water.

CFCs Chlorofluorocarbons. Gases that damage the ozone layer.

Culling To remove animals from a herd so reducing their numbers.

Disposing Throwing away.

Environment The surroundings that humans and all other animals and plants live in.

Eroded Ground down or worn away, often by the action of water, wind or ice.

Extinction When a group of animals or plants reaches the point when it has completely died out.

Fertilizers Chemicals put on the soil to help feed plants and make them grow.

Incinerators Equipment that burns up waste such as household rubbish.

Infertile When something such as soil does not produce very much.

Landscape The general scenery of a large area.

National park An area of countryside selected by the government for conservation because of its natural beauty or importance.

Natural resources Materials that we use that come from the world around us or environment.

Ozone layer A layer of gas that surrounds the Earth and protects us from harmful rays from the Sun. The ozone layer is about 20 km above the surface of the Earth.

Pesticides Chemicals used for killing pests, especially insects that damage crops.

Reserve A piece of land set aside for plants and animals.

Sewage The waste products and water that we flush down the sink, drain or toilet.

Species A group of animals or plants that are alike in most ways.

Stubble The short ends of wheat and barley left in the ground after it is cut.

Temperate A word describing parts of the world which have a mild climate.

Tropical A word describing the warm areas of the world which stretch across the Equator.

Turbine A kind of engine, usually with curved blades, turned by the action of water, steam, etc.

Books to read

Allen, S. *A Cleaner World* (Dinosaur/
Cambridge University Press, 1982)
Baines, J. *Atmosphere* (Wayland, 1991)
Bright, M. *The Dying Sea* (Franklin
Watts, 1990)

Elkington, J. & Hailes, J. *The Young
Green Consumer Guide* (Gollancz, 1990)
James, B. *Recycling* (Wayland, 1991)
Penny, M. *Pollution and Conservation*
(Wayland, 1988)

Notes for activities

Design a wildlife conservation area for part of your school grounds and discuss with your teacher how you might put it into practice. You might want to encourage animals to inhabit a pond, marshy area, wild flower meadow or a pile of logs, or grow shrubs that attract butterflies. Keep a list of all the plants and animals you find in your wild area.

Collect pictures of endangered species of wildlife from newspapers and magazines, and mount them around a map of the world. Mark where each of the animals and plants can be found. Where are most species under threat?

Find out if there are any national or international environmental projects in which you or your school can take part.

These may include checking the levels of acid rain, ground-level ozone and water quality. If possible, exchange information about your local environment with an overseas school.

Collect jars of water from a variety of places, such as a river, pond, tap, puddle or lake. Keep your hands clean by wearing rubber gloves to take water from lakes or rivers. Make a list of what you can see in each jar through a magnifying glass.

Find out all you can about schemes for recycling in your area. Find out how aluminium cans, newspapers, glass and plastic bottles are made. Make a list of the raw materials that are used to produce these and other products that we use every day.

Index

Picture acknowledgements

The publishers would like to thank the following for allowing their photographs to be used in this book: Bryan and Cherry Alexander 11; Bruce Coleman Ltd 7 top (Steven C. Kaufman), 8 (Jan Van De Kam), 13 (Dr Rocco Longo), 14 (David R. Austen); The Environmental Picture Library 9 top (Edward Parker), 19 (Michael McKinnon), 21 (V. Miles), 23 (Martin Bond), 27 (Robert Brook); Geoscience Features 10, 18 (D. Hoffman), 22; Oxford Scientific Films *front cover* (Laurence Gould), 12 (James Robinson); Photri 7 (bottom), 29; Science Photo Library *title page* (John Heseltine); Tony Stone Worldwide *back cover* (G. Brad Lewis), 4 (Peter Cade), 5 (David Woodfall), 28 (Jon Riley); Topham Picture Library 15 (Christopher Cormack); Zefa Picture Library 17 (both), 24, 26. Artwork is by Peter Bull.

SAINT BENEDICT SCHOOL
DUFFIELD ROAD
DERBY